Experiencing Chinese

Student Book
Elementary School

体验汉语®

学生用书

小学

1

高等教育出版社
Higher Education Press

MW01071310

致小朋友

亲爱的小朋友们：

　　你们知道吗，在亚洲的东部有一个国家叫做"中国"。跟你们国家一样，中国有很多好玩儿的地方，有很多好吃的食物，也有很多有趣的动物和植物。在这里，北方的冬天会下雪，南方的昆明则四季如春；东北的森林里生活着东北虎，西南的森林里生活着大熊猫；北方人喜欢吃咸一点儿的菜，西南地区的人喜欢吃特别辣的菜。总之，关于中国，有趣的事情几天几夜也说不完。

　　世界上有许多国家，不同国家的人们说着不一样的语言，写着不一样的文字。中国人说的语言叫做"汉语"，写的文字叫做"汉字"。如果你们想认识中国的小朋友，或者长大后来中国旅游、学习，那么就要会说一点儿汉语。有了这本书，你们现在就可以开始体验汉语学习的快乐之旅。在这次旅程中，你们将学习汉语的发音、文字、词语和句子，也可以跟老师、同学们一起唱歌、做游戏、做手工。

　　非常感谢中国国家汉办的叔叔阿姨们，在他们的支持和许多人的共同努力下，我们终于完成了这本书。我们希望它能成为联系世界各国小朋友友谊的纽带。愿它成为你们开启汉语世界大门、体验中国的一把金钥匙。

体验汉语，体验快乐，体验中国！

国际语言研究与发展中心

2008年7月

To The Children

Dear Children,

Do you know there is a country that lies in East Asia whose name is "China"? The same as in your country, China has many good places to play, has a lot of delicious food to eat, and also has lots of interesting animals and plants. It snows during the winter in the northern part of China. While in Kunming, in the southern part, it's like spring all year round. In the forest of the northeast, there lives the Northeast Tiger. In the forest of the southwest, there are giant pandas. The people who live in the north like salty food. The people who live in the southwest prefer spicy food. In a word, with regard to China, you can't finish telling its interesting stories in just a few days and nights.

There are many countries in the world. Different people from different countries speak different languages and write differently. The language that the Chinese people speak is called "Hànyǔ." The characters they write are called "Hànzì." If you want to get to know Chinese kids, or you want to travel and study in China when you grow up, you need to know some Chinese. With this book, you can experience the interesting journey of learning Chinese, right now! During your travels, you will learn Chinese pronunciation, characters, words, and sentences. You can also sing with your teacher and classmates, play games, do handicrafts, and so on.

Many thanks to the staff of the National Office of Teaching Chinese as a Foreign Language. With their support and that of many other people working together, we were able to finish this book. We hope this book becomes a bond of friendship that binds together children from all over the world. May it become a door that leads you to the Chinese language world, and become a golden key to experiencing China.

Experiencing Chinese, Experiencing Happiness and Experiencing Success!

International Language Research and Development Center

July, 2008

Useful Expressions	Sentences	Characters
1.老师好！　2.你好！		
	这/那 是……	十　王
1.你好！/你们好！　2.我叫……		
	她是……	八　人
1.你几岁？　2.我九岁。		
	我的……	木　本
1.再见！		
		六　下
1.谢谢！　2.不客气。/不用谢。		
	现在……点（半）	大　太
1.对不起！　2.没关系。/没事儿。		
	……有……	小　丁
1.欢迎你！　2.请进！　3.谢谢！		
	我喜欢……	火　父
1.请坐。/请喝水。　2.谢谢！		
	我爱……	不　手

第 1 课 动 物
dòng wù

Let's read 读一读

Aa

ā á ǎ à

ai   ao   an   ang

Exercises 练一练

Listen and choose. 听录音，选一选。

·ā	·āi	·āo	·ān	·āng
·á	·ái	·áo	·án	·áng
·ǎ	·ǎi	·ǎo	·ǎn	·ǎng
·à	·ài	·ào	·àn	·àng

Activity 课堂活动

Find, arrange the *Pinyin* cards, and compete. 找一找，拼卡片，比一比。

Listen to the teacher, and arrange the *Pinyin* cards with your partners.
听老师读拼音，和你的同伴一起拼卡片。

Animals

Let's remember 认一认

猫
māo

狗
gǒu

大 象
dàxiàng

鱼
yú

鸟
niǎo

熊 猫
xióngmāo

这 zhè this　　　那 nà that　　　是 shì to be

Exercises　练一练

1 **Complete the pictures and match.**　完成图画并连线。

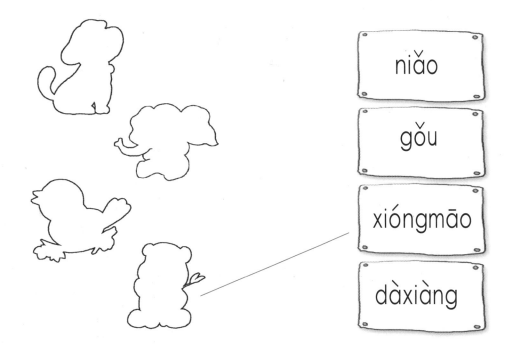

niǎo

gǒu

xióngmāo

dàxiàng

2 **Listen and choose.**　听录音，选一选。

Activity 课堂活动

Draw and color. 描一描，涂一涂。

What animals do you and your partners like? Let your partners color the *Pinyin*, and you color the pictures.
你和你的同伴都喜欢什么动物？让同伴描出它们的拼音，你为动物涂上颜色吧！

Let's say 说一说

第 2 课 这是狗
zhè shì gǒu

Let's learn 学一学

2 那 是 猫。
Nà shì māo.

1 这 是 狗。
Zhè shì gǒu.

dàxiàng

xióngmāo

yú

niǎo

Zhè shì gǒu.
Zhè shì gǒu.
Gǒu gǒu gǒu gǒu.
Zhè shì gǒu.

Nà shì māo.
Nà shì māo.
Māo māo māo māo.
Nà shì māo.

Zhè shì yú.
Zhè shì yú.
Yú yú yú yú.
Zhè shì yú.

Nà shì niǎo.
Nà shì niǎo.
Niǎo niǎo niǎo niǎo.
Nà shì niǎo.

Exercises 练一练

Choose and write. 选一选，写一写。

这
zhè
是
shì
鸟
niǎo
那
nà
猫
māo

zhè

nà

_____ shì niǎo.

_____ shì niǎo.

_____ shì māo.

_____ shì māo.

2

This is a dog

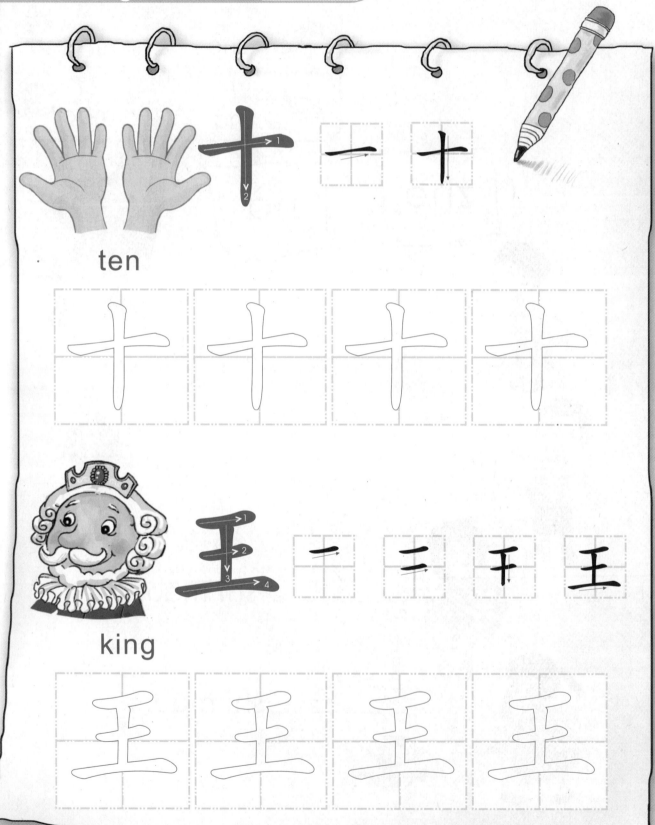

ten

king

Let's do it 做一做

这是熊猫。
These are pandas.

它们生活在中国。
They live in China.

它们吃竹子。
They eat bamboo shoots.

一起做个熊猫面具吧。 (见125页)

Let's make a panda mask (see P125)

Let's draw 画一画

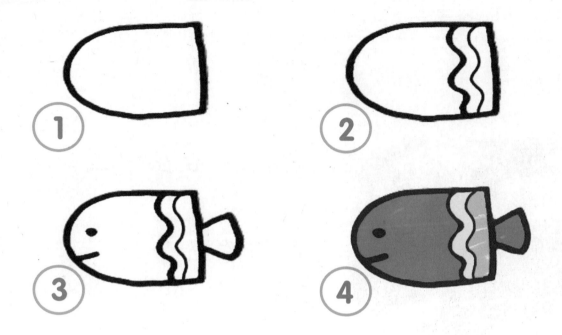

Everyone draw a stroke and let's see what picture you can draw together.
和你的同伴每人画一笔，看看最后画出的是什么？

Story time　故事会

第 3 课 人物

rén wù

Let's read 读一读

ou   ong

Exercises 练一练

Listen and mark the tones. 听录音，写声调。

ǒ

o

ou

ǒu

ong

ong

Activity 课堂活动

3

Persons

Get the ball, then read the *Pinyin*. 接皮球，读拼音。

After you get the ball, let your partner read the *Pinyin*.
接到球以后，让你的同伴读出拼音。

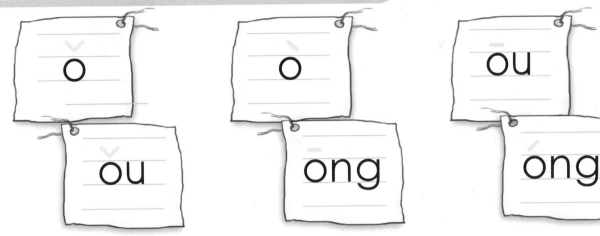

1 ōu

2 ōu

Let's remember 认一认

你
nǐ

我
wǒ

她
tā

他
tā

姐 姐
jiějie

妹 妹
mèimei

老 师
lǎoshī

学 生
xuésheng

Exercises 练一练

1 Match. 连线。

she/he

I

you

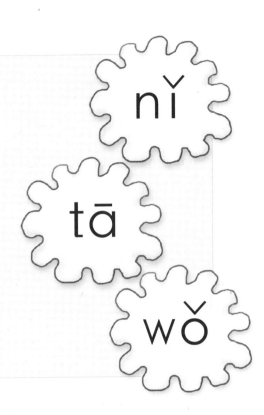

nǐ

tā

wǒ

2 Listen and read. 听读。

① ② ③

3

Find and color. 找一找，涂一涂。

Find and color the syllables with your partner to see who can get more words.
和你的同伴一起找音节并涂色，看谁找出的词语多。

c	m	z	w	ü	q	h	x	l
y	c	d	o	f	j	x	u	n
d	h	j	m	e	i	m	e	i
k	z	e	u	o	e	l	s	o
u	t	w	s	l	j	d	h	w
l	a	o	s	h	i	ü	e	c
j	x	a	c	ü	e	f	n	k
o	n	e	y	o	a	q	g	s

你们 好! 我 叫 元 元。
Nǐmen hǎo! Wǒ jiào Yuányuan.
Hello, everyone. My name is Yuanyuan.

3

Persons

你 好! 我 叫 丁 丁。
1 **Nǐ hǎo! Wǒ jiào Dīngding.**
Hello. My name is Dingding.

你 好! 我 叫 丽丽。
2 **Nǐ hǎo! Wǒ jiào Lìli.**
Hello. My name is Lili.

第 **4** 课

她 是 妹妹
tā shì mèi mei

你 是 姐 姐。
Nǐ shì jiějie. **1**

她 是 妹 妹。
Tā shì mèimei. **2**

wǒ

lǎoshī

tā

xuésheng

Sing and guess 唱一唱，猜一猜

Nǐ shì Dīngding.

Nǐ shì Dīngding.

Shì xuésheng, shì xuésheng.

Nǐ shì Dūyà.

Nǐ shì Dūyà.

Shì xuésheng, shì xuésheng.

我们是谁?

Who are we?

Nǐ shì Dīngding.

Exercises 练一练

Write your name and the names of your friends. 写出自己和朋友们的名字。

我 wǒ		老 师
你 nǐ	是	lǎoshī
他 tā	shì	学 生
她 tā		xuésheng

Wǒ shì _____.

Nǐ shì _____.

Tā shì _____.

Tā shì _____.

4

She is the younger sister

Interesting characters 趣味汉字

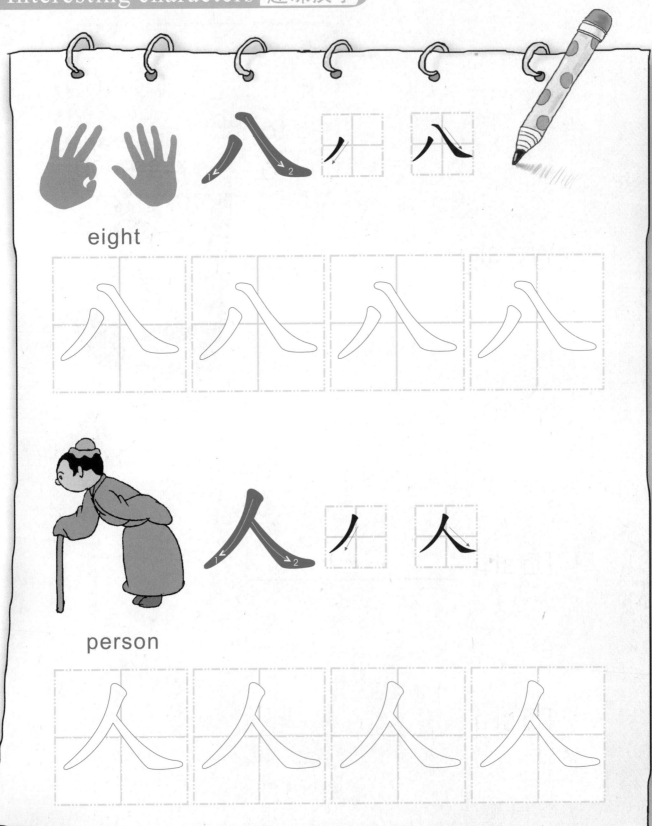

eight

person

Wǒ shì Dīngding.
Wǒ shì xuésheng.

Zhōngguó China

Běijīng Beijing

关于我自己 About myself

4

She is the younger sister

31

Walk and write 走一走，写一写

nà shì

nà shì

shì lǎoshī

shì xuésheng

zhè shì

shì mèimei

Story time 故事会

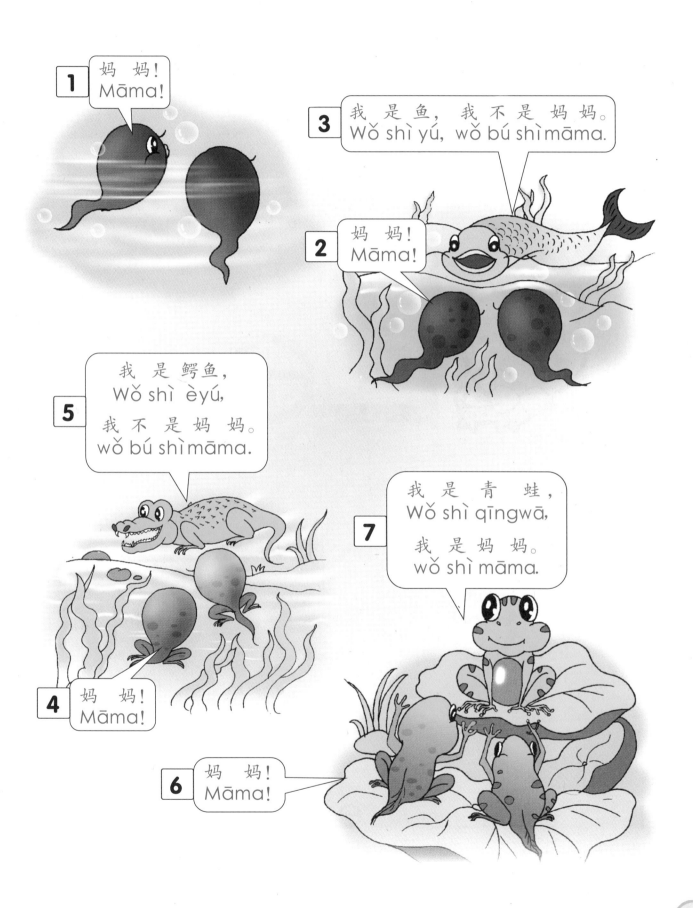

第 5 课 衣服
yī fu

Ee

ē   é   ě   è

ei   en   eng   er

34

Exercises 练一练

Listen and number the pictures. 听录音，填序号。

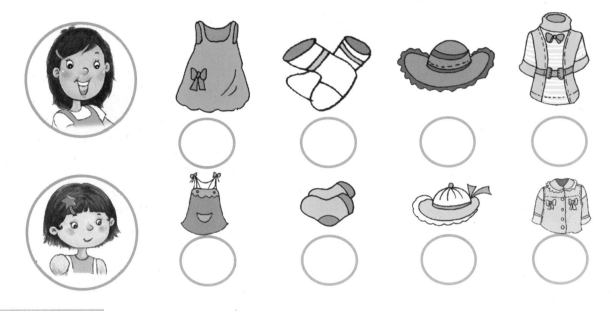

Activity 课堂活动

Write and read. 写一写，读一读。

上 衣
shàngyī

鞋
xié

裙 子
qúnzi

裤子
kùzi

袜子
wàzi

帽 子
màozi

看 **kàn** look

的 **de** of

Exercises 练一练

1 Choose. 选一选。

- shāngyī
- shāngyì
- shàngyī

- kùzi
- kùzǐ
- kūzì

- wázi
- wàzi
- wāzi

- xiè
- xiě
- xié

2 Listen and number the pictures. 听录音，填序号。

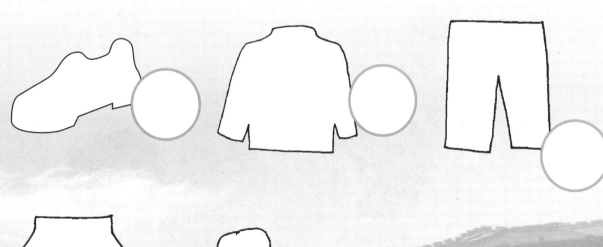

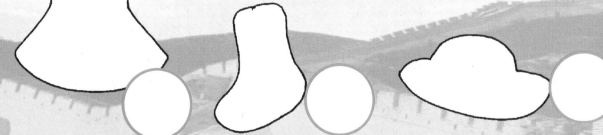

Activity 课堂活动

Spin, read, and point. 转一转，读一读，指一指。

第**6**课 我的鞋
wǒ de xié

Let's learn 学一学

1 看！他的帽子。
Kàn! Tā de màozi.

2 看！我的鞋。
Kàn! Wǒ de xié.

40

wǒ de kùzi

wǒ de qúnzi

tā de wàzi

tā de shàngyī

Zhè shì shàngyī.

Zhè shì shàngyī.

Lā lā lā lā lā lā.

Zhè shì nǐ de shàngyī.

Zhè shì nǐ de shàngyī.

Lā lā lā lā lā lā.

Exercises 练一练

Choose and write. 选一选，写一写。

我 wǒ		
你 nǐ	的	帽子
他 tā	de	màozi
老师 lǎoshī		

Zhè shì _____.

Zhè shì _____.

Zhè shì _____.

Zhè shì _____.

6

My shoes

43

Interesting characters 趣味汉字

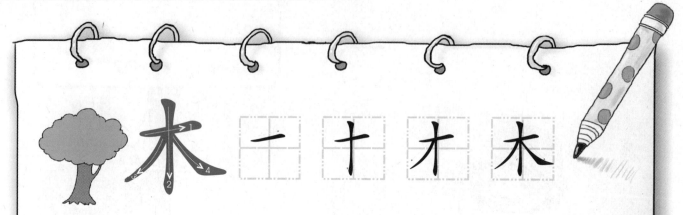

tree

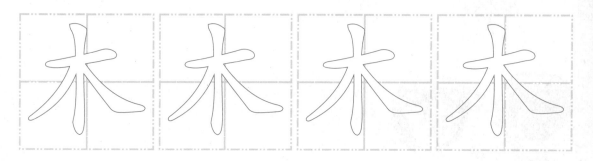

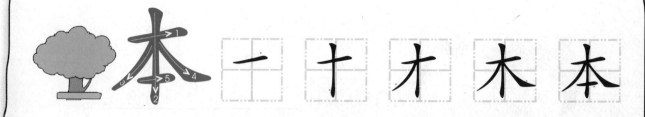

base

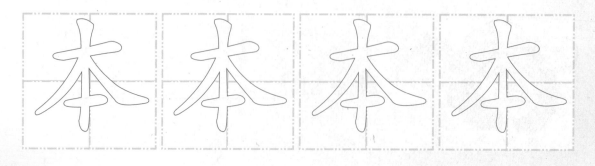

Do you know? 你知道吗？

为老师画一幅像吧！

Draw a picture for your teacher!

中国
Zhōngguó

China

泰国
Tàiguó

Thailand

6

My shoes

日本
Rìběn

Japan

韩国
Hánguó

South Korea

Draw, cut, and fit together the puzzle
画一画，剪一剪，拼一拼

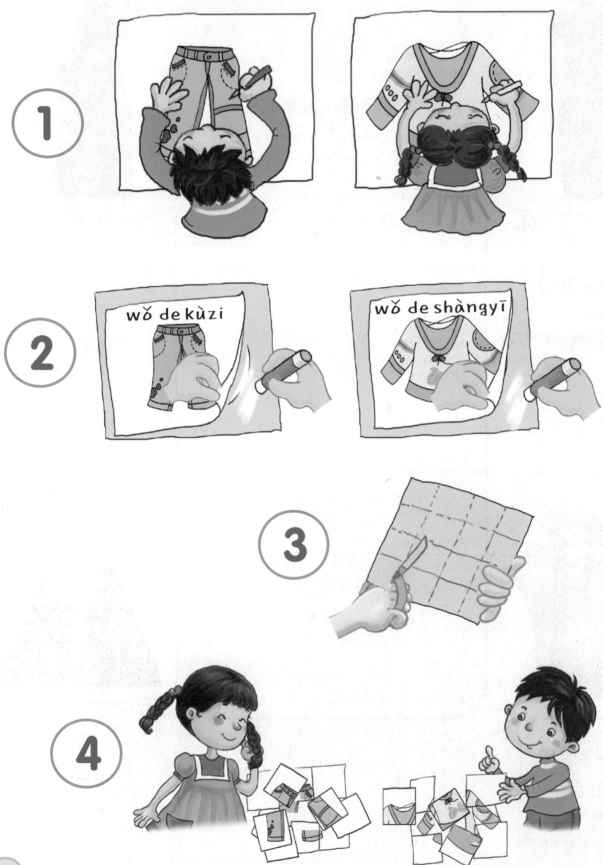

Story time　故事会

第 **7** 课 数字 **2**
shù zì

Let's read 读一读

ī   í   ǐ   ì

iu   ie   in   ing

Exercises 练一练

Listen and choose. 听录音，选一选。

1 • iú • iù
2 • iē • iě
3 • ǐn • ìn

4 • iù • iè
5 • ǐn • ǐng
6 • iū • īn

Activity 课堂活动

Listen and point. 听一听，指一指。

7

Numbers

49

Let's remember 认一认

一
yī

二
èr

三
sān

四
sì

五
wǔ

六
liù

七
qī

八
bā

Exercises 练一练

1 Choose. 选一选。

 yī èr

 sì èr

sān yī

wǔ sì

2 Listen and choose. 听录音，选一选。

① •354 •345 •374

② •482 •382 •328

③ •5677 •5766 •5767

④ •3254 •2345 •2354

Activity 课堂活动

Find and count. 找一找，数一数。

māo	niǎo	gǒu

xuésheng	lǎoshī	xióngmāo

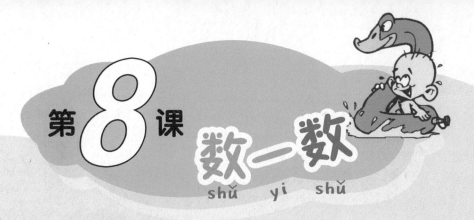

第 8 课 数一数
shǔ yi shǔ

8

Yī èr sān, sān èr yī.

Yī èr sān sì wǔ liù qī.

Yī èr sān, sān èr yī.

Qī liù wǔ sì sān èr yī.

Yī èr sān, sān èr yī.

Yī èr sān sì wǔ liù qī.

Yī èr sān, sān èr yī.

Qī liù wǔ sì sān èr yī.

Exercises 练一练

Find the differences. 找不同。

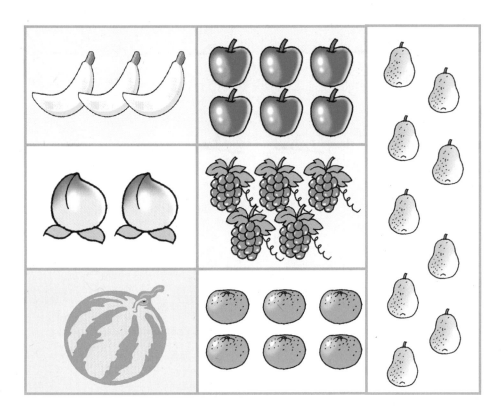

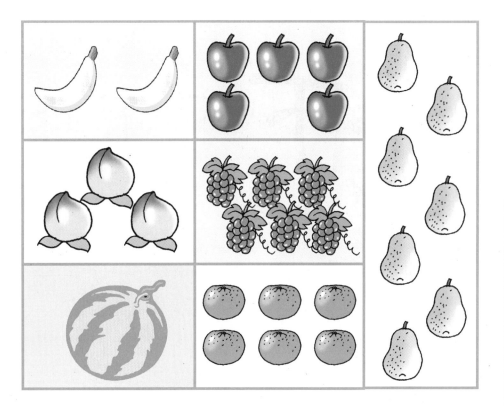

Chinese XP®

8
Count it

57

Interesting characters 趣味汉字

六 ` 一 亠 六 六

six

下 一 丁 下

under

Do you know? 你知道吗？

Numbers in life 生活中的数字

Please draw some thing related to the numbers according to the examples.
根据例子，画出跟数字有关的事物。

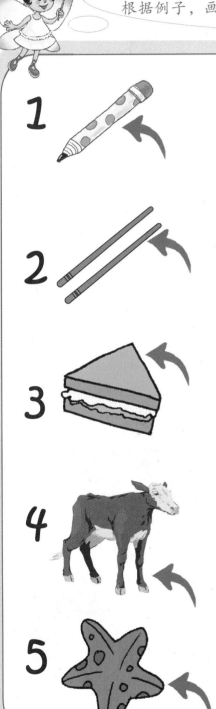

1

2

3

4

5

Throw, walk, and count 扔一扔，走一走，数一数

Play with your partners and see who is the winner. Remember to fill in the blanks with the numbers, otherwise you must go back to the jumping-off point.

和你的同伴一起玩。看看谁能先到终点。每个袋子上边都要填上正确的数字，否则就要从头开始哦！

Story time 故事会

Let's read 读一读

U u

ū ú ǔ ù

ui   un

62

Chinese XP

Exercises 练一练

Listen and color. 听录音，涂一涂。

1 āi ēi īu uī

2 áo óu iú uí

3 àn èn ìn ùn

4 āng ēng īng ōng

9 Time

Activity 课堂活动

Listen and speak. 听一听，传一传。

Pass the *Pinyin* you heard to the next student.
把你听到的拼音小声地传给后面的同学。

① uì

②

③

uì

63

9

Let's remember 认一认

九 jiǔ
9

两 liǎng
2

十 shí
10

十一 shíyī
11

十二 shí'èr
12

半 bàn

现在 xiànzài now

点 diǎn o'clock

64

Exercises 练一练

1 Listen and number the time. 听录音，填序号。

2:00

9:00

10:30

12:30

2 Read and choose. 读一读，选一选。

	一 yī	
现在 xiànzài	两 liǎng	点 diǎn
	三 sān	

- Xiànzài sān diǎn.
- Xiànzài sān diǎn bàn.

- Xiànzài sì diǎn.
- Xiànzài sì diǎn bàn.

- Xiànzài shí'èr diǎn.
- Xiànzài liù diǎn.

- Xiànzài shí'yī diǎn bàn.
- Xiànzài shí'èr diǎn bàn.

Activity 课堂活动

Ask and write. 问一问，写一写。

Make a timetable for your partner.
给你的同伴做一张作息表吧。

Name: _____

qǐ chuáng	_____ : _____	点
chī zǎofàn	_____ : _____	点
shàngkè	_____ : _____	点
fàngxué	_____ : _____	点
chī wǎnfàn	_____ : _____	点
shuìjiào	_____ : _____	点

现在两点
xiàn zài liǎng diǎn

Let's learn 学一学

1 现在 两 点。
Xiànzài liǎng diǎn.

2 现在九点半。
Xiànzài jiǔ diǎn bàn.

shí diǎn

shíyī diǎn bàn

shí'èr diǎn

Sing and play a game 唱一唱，做游戏

Xiànzài yī diǎn.

Xiànzài yī diǎn.

Xiànzài yī diǎn.

Yī yī yī.

Xiànzài sān diǎn.

Xiànzài sān diǎn.

Xiànzài sān diǎn.

Sān sān sān.

Exercises 练一练

Look and write. 看一看，写一写。

1 Lúndūn
London

2 Niǔyuē
New York

3 Běijīng
Beijing

4 Dōngjīng
Tokyo

5 Bālí
Paris

6 Xīní
Sidney

1  ____点
diǎn

2 ____点
diǎn

3 ____点
diǎn

4  ____点
diǎn

5 ____点
diǎn

6 ____点
diǎn

Interesting characters 趣味汉字

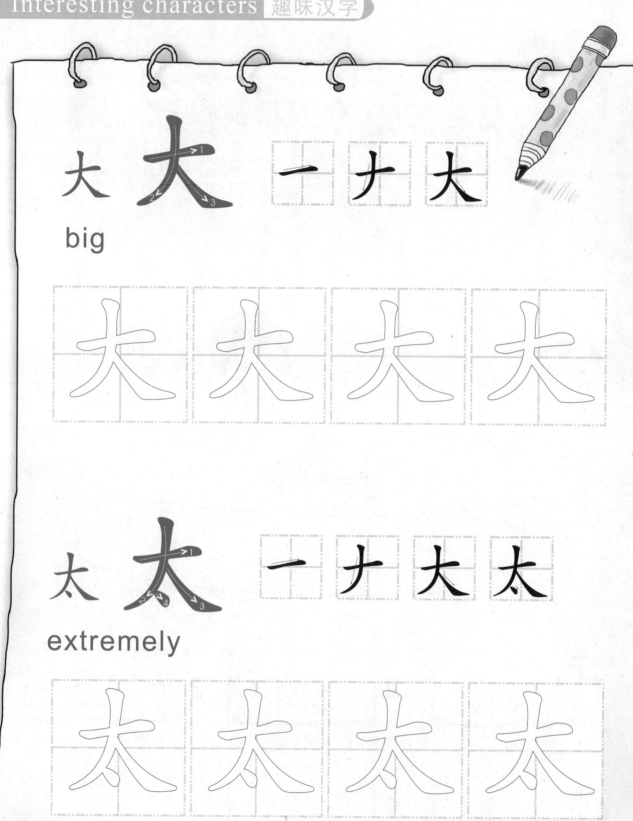

大 大 一 ナ 大

big

大 大 大 大

太 太 一 ナ 大 太

extremely

太 太 太 太

Find the differences 找不同

Two students in one group. Let's see which group can find the six differences first.

两个人一组，看看哪一组找得又快又准确。

DIY a clock , spin, and talk 自制钟表，转一转，说一说

现在 三 点。
Xiànzài sān diǎn.

Story time 故事会

第 11 课 身体
shēn tǐ

Let's read 读一读

ü

ǖ ǘ ǚ ǜ

üe   ün

Exercises 练一练

Listen and mark the tones. 听录音，写声调。

Activity 课堂活动

Listen and raise the cards. 听一听，举卡片。

Body

Let's remember 认一认

翅 膀
chìbǎng

眼 睛
yǎnjing

耳 朵
ěrduo

鼻子
bízi

尾 巴
wěiba

脚
jiǎo

有 yǒu have/has

Exercises 练一练

1 Listen and number the parts of the picture. 听录音，填序号。

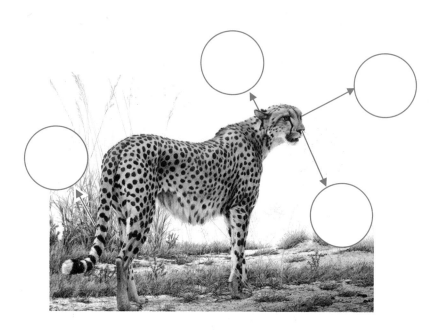

2 Listen and choose. 听录音，选一选。

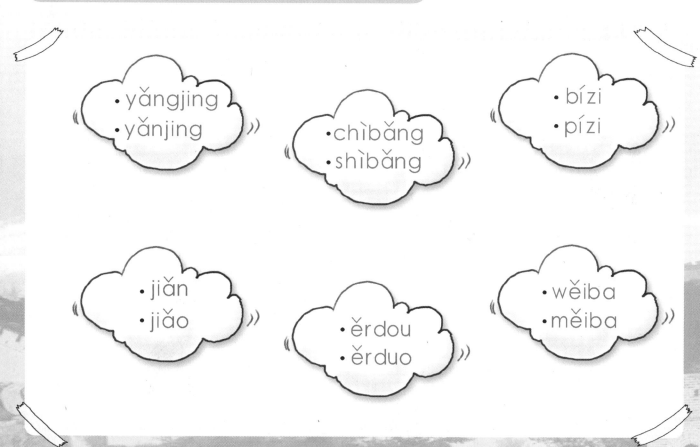

- yǎngjing
- yǎnjing

- chìbǎng
- shìbǎng

- bízi
- pízi

- jiǎn
- jiǎo

- ěrdou
- ěrduo

- wěiba
- měiba

Activity 课堂活动

Speak, listen, and point. 说一说，听一听，指一指。

Listen and draw. 听一听，画一画。

1 对不起。
Duìbuqǐ.
Sorry.

2 没关系。
Méiguānxi.
No problem.

11 Body

1 对不起。
Duìbuqǐ.
Sorry.

2 没事儿。
Méi shìr.
No problem.

鸟有翅膀
niǎo yǒu chì bǎng

鸟 有 翅 膀。
Niǎo yǒu chìbǎng.

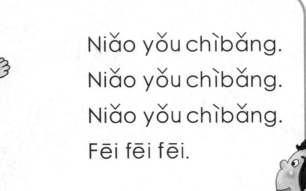

Niǎo yǒu chìbǎng.
Niǎo yǒu chìbǎng.
Niǎo yǒu chìbǎng.
Fēi fēi fēi.

Yú yǒu wěiba.
Yú yǒu wěiba.
Yú yǒu wěiba.
Yóu yóu yóu.

Gǒu yǒu bízi.
Gǒu yǒu bízi.
Gǒu yǒu bízi.
Wén wén wén.

Dàxiàng yǒu jiǎo.
Dàxiàng yǒu jiǎo.
Dàxiàng yǒu jiǎo.
Zǒu zǒu zǒu.

Exercises 练一练

Read and write. 读一读，写一写。

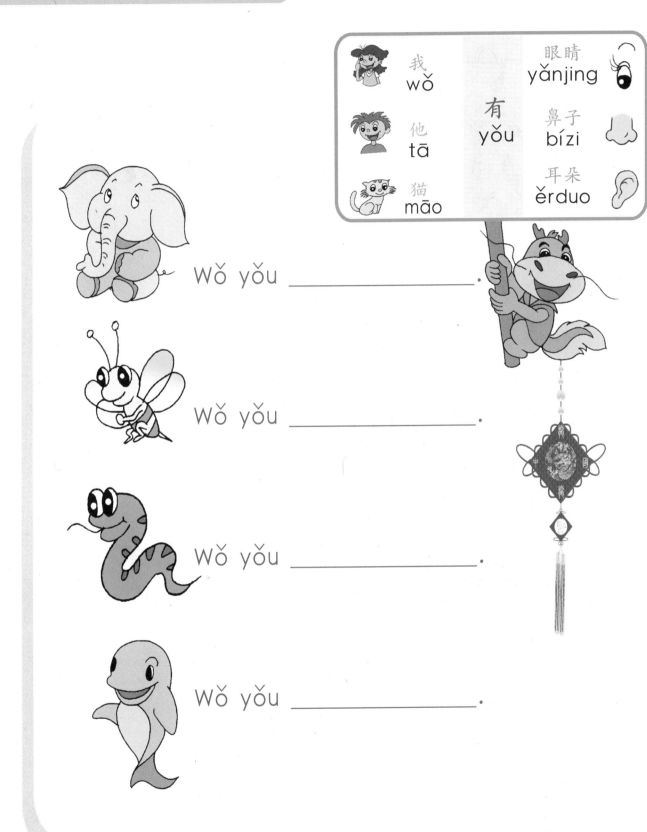

我 wǒ		眼睛 yǎnjing	
他 tā	有 yǒu	鼻子 bízi	
猫 māo		耳朵 ěrduo	

Wǒ yǒu _____.

Wǒ yǒu _____.

Wǒ yǒu _____.

Wǒ yǒu _____.

12

Birds have wings

85

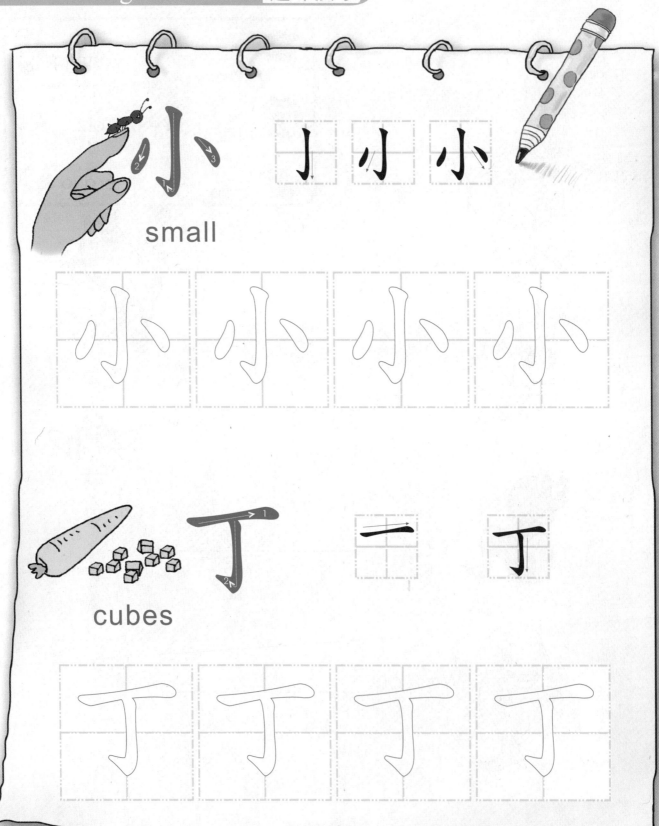

small

cubes

Do you know? 你知道吗?

Men's feet and animals' feet are different. Look and think, what's the function of our feet?
人和动物的脚长得不一样，名称也不一样。看一看，想一想，人的脚可以用来做什么？

12

Birds have wings

87

Review 6

Throw and speak 扔一扔，说一说

鸟 有 翅膀。
Niǎo yǒu chìbǎng.

Story time 故事会

第 13 课 颜色
yán sè

Let's read 读一读

b p m f d t n l g k h

a o e i u ü

Exercises 练一练

Listen and color. 听录音，涂一涂。

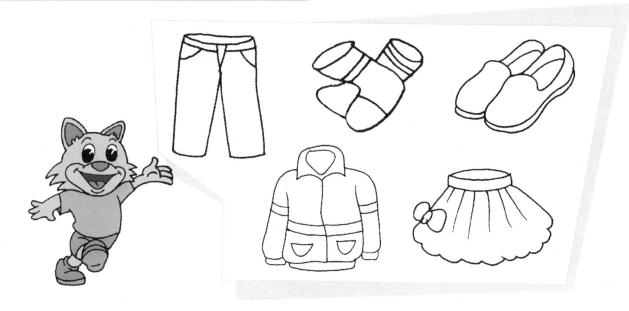

Activity 课堂活动

Get one card and let your partner read it. 抽一张卡片，请你的同伴读一读。

Let's remember 认一认

红 色
hóngsè

白 色
báisè

蓝色
lánsè

黑色
hēisè

黄 色
huángsè

绿色
lǜsè

喜欢　xǐhuan　like

Exercises 练一练

1 Choose. 选一选。

- huángsè   • lánsè   • huángsè   • hēisè

- hóngsè   • lùsè   • lánsè   • báisè

2 Match. 连线。

hóngsè

lánsè

lùsè

huángsè

báisè

hēisè

13

Activity 课堂活动

Say out one color you like. Look around with your classmates and find the things with this color. Find out who is fast!

说一种你喜欢的颜色，然后和同学们一起找一找有没有这种颜色。看谁找得快！

我喜欢红色。
Wǒ xǐhuan hóngsè.

红色！
Hóngsè!

94

第 14 课 我喜欢红色
wǒ xǐ huan hóng sè

Let's learn 学一学

我 喜 欢 红 色。
Wǒ xǐhuan hóngsè.

báisè

hēisè

lánsè

huángsè

lùsè

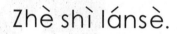

Zhè shì lánsè.

Zhè shì lánsè.

Lán lán lán lán lán lán.

Wǒ xǐhuan lánsè.

Wǒ xǐhuan lánsè.

Lán lán lán lán lán lán.

Exercises 练一练

Read and write. 读一读，写一写。

我 wǒ		绿色 lǜsè
他 tā	喜 欢 xǐhuan	蓝色 lánsè
老师 lǎoshī		黑色 hēisè

Wǒ xǐhuan_____.

Tā xǐhuan_____.

Wǒ xǐhuan_____.

Tā xǐhuan_____.

Lǎoshī xǐhuan_____.

14

I like red color

99

fire

火　火　火　火

father

七巧板 Tangram

见127页(See P127)

14

I like red color

Choose and color   选一选，涂一涂

Let your partner write down the name of his/her favorite color after the number, then you color the clown together.

让你的同伴在数字后面写上他喜欢的颜色的名称，然后你们一起为小丑涂上颜色吧。

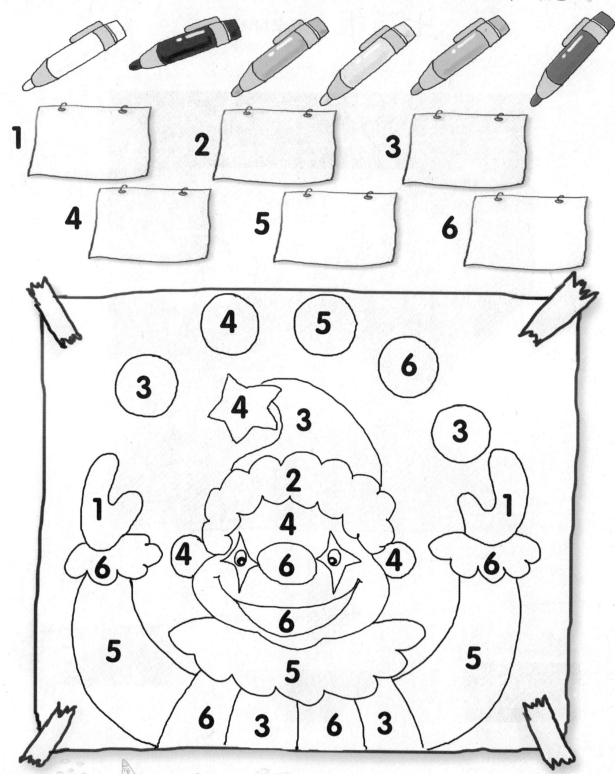

Story time 故事会

第 15 课 家人

jiā rén

Let's read 读一读

j q x z c s r zh ch sh y w

a o e i u ü

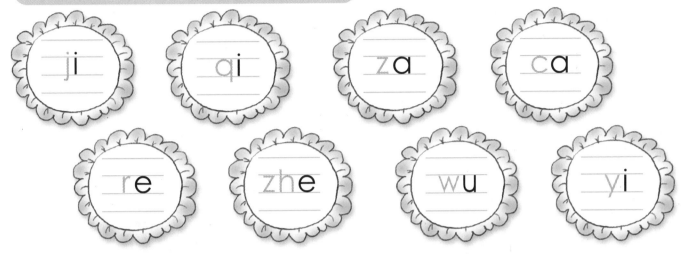

Exercises 练一练

Listen and write. 听一听，写一写。

ji   qi   za   ca

re   zhe   wu   yi

Activity 课堂活动

Spell and speak. 拼一拼，说一说。

Let's remember 认一认

爸爸 bàba

妈妈 māma

爷爷 yéye

哥哥 gēge

奶奶 nǎinai

弟弟 dìdi

爱 ài love

Exercises 练一练

1 Match. 连线。

yéye   dìdi   māma   gēge   nǎinai   bàba

2 Listen and number the picture. 听录音，填序号。

15

How many people are there in your family? Please draw a picture of your family on a piece of white paper.
你家里有什么人？请在白纸上画一幅家庭关系图。

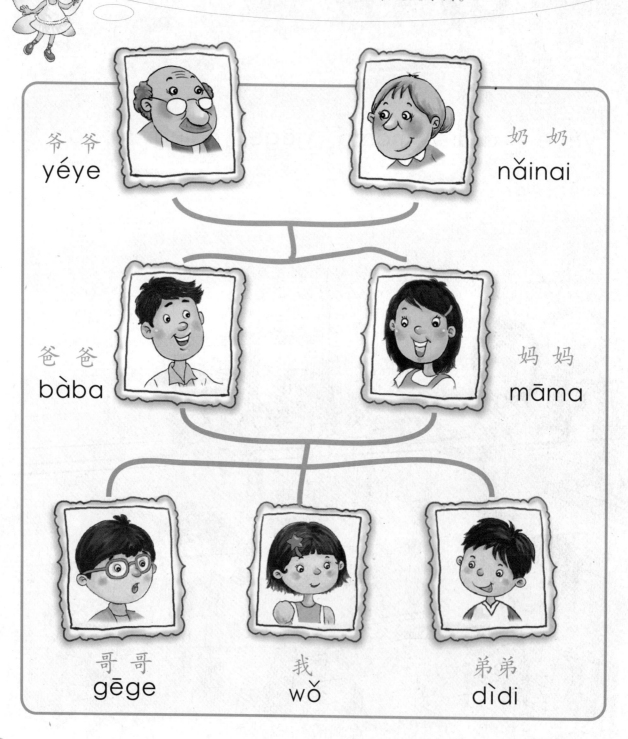

爷爷 yéye

奶奶 nǎinai

爸爸 bàba

妈妈 māma

哥哥 gēge

我 wǒ

弟弟 dìdi

1 请 坐。
Qǐng zuò.
Take your seat, please.

2 谢 谢!
Xièxie!
Thank you!

1 请 喝 水。
Qǐng hē shuǐ.
Have some water, please.

2 谢 谢!
Xièxie!
Thank you!

15

Family members

我爱妈妈
wǒ ài mā ma

yéye

nǎinai

bàba

gēge

dìdi

Bàba bàba hǎo bàba.
Wǒ ài hǎo bàba.

Māma māma hǎo māma.
Wǒ ài hǎo māma.

Nǎinai nǎinai hǎo nǎinai.
Wǒ ài hǎo nǎinai.

Yéye yéye hǎo yéye.
Wǒ ài hǎo yéye.

Exercises 练一练

Paste photos and say. 贴照片，说一说。

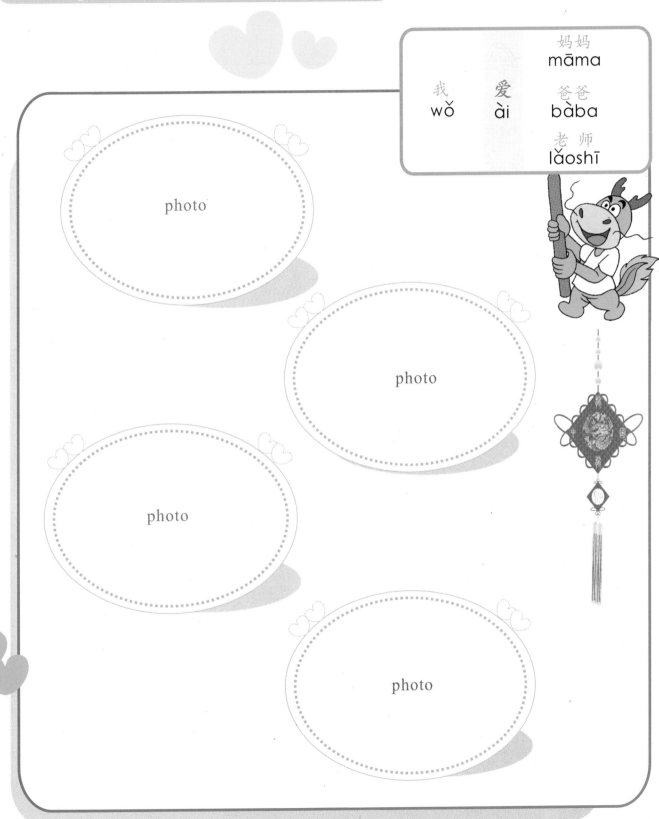

		妈妈 māma
我 wǒ	爱 ài	爸爸 bàba
		老师 lǎoshī

16

I love mom

photo

photo

photo

photo

一 丁 丌 不

no/not

不 不 不 不

一 二 三 手

hand

手 手 手 手

Let's do it 做一做

给妈妈做张卡片 Make a card for your mom

妈妈,
　　我爱你!

Write and guess 写一写，猜一猜

Write down your family members' names, then ask your partner to guess who they are.

写出你家人的名字，请你的同伴猜一猜他们都是谁。

1 他是你 的爸爸。
Tā shì nǐ de bàba.

2 是。他是我 的爸爸。
Shì. Tā shì wǒ de bàba.

Story time 故事会

Wordlist
词语表

A

| 爱 | ài | love | 15 |

B

八	bā	eight	7
爸爸	bàba	dad	15
白色	báisè	white	13
半	bàn	half	9
鼻子	bízi	nose	11

C

| 翅膀 | chìbǎng | wing | 11 |
| 大象 | dàxiàng | elephant | 1 |

D

的	de	of	5
弟弟	dìdi	younger brother	15
点	diǎn	o'clock	9

E

| 耳朵 | ěrduo | ear | 11 |
| 二 | èr | two | 7 |

G

| 哥哥 | gēge | older brother | 15 |

狗	gǒu	dog	1

黑色	hēisè	black	13
红色	hóngsè	red	13
黄色	huángsè	yellow	13

脚	jiǎo	foot	11
姐姐	jiějie	older sister	3
九	jiǔ	nine	9

看	kàn	look	5
裤子	kùzi	pants	5

蓝色	lánsè	blue	13
老师	lǎoshī	teacher	3
两	liǎng	two	9
六	liù	six	7
绿色	lǜsè	green	13

妈妈	māma	mom	15
猫	māo	cat	1
帽子	màozi	hat	5
妹妹	mèimei	younger sister	3

Answer

第1课　动物

听录音，选一选。
　á　ài　ǎo　ān　áng

1. 完成图画并连线。

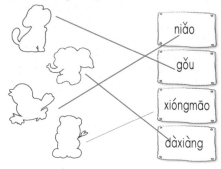

　niǎo
　gǒu
　xióngmāo
　dàxiàng

2. 听录音，选一选。

第2课　这是狗

选一选，写一写。
　zhè　nà　zhè　nà

第3课　人物

听录音，写声调。
　ǒ　ò　ōu　ǒu　ōng　óng

连线。
　she/he——tā　I——wǒ　you——nǐ

找一找，涂一涂。
　wo　laoshi　jiejie　meimei　ni

复习2

走一走，写一写。
　nǐ shì mèimei　　zhè shì gǒu
　wǒ shì xuésheng　nà shì niǎo
　tā shì lǎoshī　　nà shì xióngmāo

第5课　衣服

听录音，填序号。

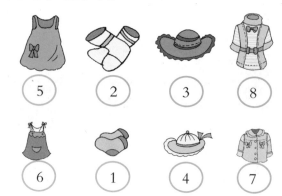

录音文本：
1. 妹妹的袜子　　2. 姐姐的袜子
3. 姐姐的帽子　　4. 妹妹的帽子
5. 姐姐的裙子　　6. 妹妹的裙子
7. 妹妹的上衣　　8. 姐姐的上衣

1. 选一选。
　shàngyī　kùzi　wàzi　xié

2. 听录音，填序号。

录音文本：
1. 帽子　　2. 裤子　　3. 裙子
4. 鞋　　　5. 上衣　　6. 袜子

第6课　我的鞋

读一读，写一写。
Zhè shì wǒ de màozi.
Zhè shì nǐ de màozi.
Zhè shì tā de màozi.
Zhè shì lǎoshī/tā de màozi.

第7课　数字

听录音，选一选。
1. iú　2. iě　3. ǐn　4. iù　5. ǐng　6. īn

1. 选一选。
yī　èr　sān　sì

2. 听录音，选一选。
1. 354　2. 382　3. 5767　4. 3254

找一找，数一数。
māo 3　　　niǎo 6　　　gǒu 2
xuésheng 3　　lǎoshī 1　　xióngmāo 1

复习4

扔一扔，走一走，数一数。

3　　2　　6　　2
3　　4　　8　　8
4　　5　　4　　7
1　　2　　6

第9课　时间

听录音，涂一涂。
1. ēi　2. óu　3. ìn　4. ōng

1. 听录音，填序号。
3　1　4　2

录音文本：
1. 九点　2. 十二点半　3. 两点　4. 十点半

2. 看一看，选一选。
1. Xiànzài sān diǎn
2. Xiànzài sì diǎn
3. Xiànzàii liù diǎn
4. Xiànzài shíyī diǎn bàn

第10课　现在两点

看一看，写一写。
1. 12点　2. 7点　3. 8点
4. 7点　5. 1点　6. 10点

第11课　身体

听录音，填序号。

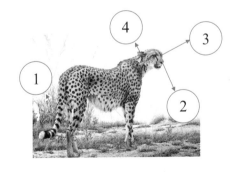

录音文本：
1.尾巴　2.鼻子　3.眼睛　4.耳朵

1. 听录音，标出声调。
ú　ǔ　yuē　yuè　yún　yùn

2. 听录音，选一选。
    1. yǎnjing   2. chìbǎng   3. bízi
    4. jiǎo   5. ěrduo   6. wěiba

第13课　颜色

听录音，涂一涂。

录音文本：
红色的裤子　绿色的袜子　黑色的鞋
黄色的上衣　蓝色的裙子

选一选。
   hóngsè　lánsè　huángsè　báisè

第14课　我喜欢红色

读一读，写一写。
   huángsè   lánsè   lùsè
   hēisè   hóngsè

第15课　家人

连线。

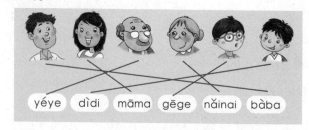

yéye　dìdi　māma　gēge　nǎinai　bàba

听录音，填序号。

录音文本：
1. 爷爷   2. 弟弟   3. 妈妈
4. 奶奶   5. 爸爸   6. 哥哥

熊猫面具 Panda mask

郑 重 声 明

图书在版编目（CIP）数据

体验汉语小学学生用书. 第1册 / 国际语言研究与发展
中心. —北京：高等教育出版社，2008.8
　ISBN 978-7-04-022269-2

　Ⅰ. 体… Ⅱ. 国… Ⅲ. 汉语－对外汉语教学－教材
Ⅳ. H195.4

　中国版本图书馆CIP数据核字（2008）第119831号

策划编辑 周　芳　**责任编辑** 周　芳　**责任印制** 陈伟光

出版发行	高等教育出版社	购书热线	010-58581118
社　　址	北京市西城区德外大街 4 号	免费咨询	800-810-0598
邮政编码	100120	网　　址	http://www.hep.edu.cn
总　　机	010-58581000		http://www.hep.com.cn
经　　销	蓝色畅想图书发行有限公司	网上订购	http://www.landraco.com
			http://www.landraco.com.cn
印　　刷	涿州市星河印刷有限公司	畅想教育	http://www.widedu.com
开　　本	889×1194　1/16	版　　次	2008 年 8 月第 1 版
印　　张	8.25	印　　次	2008 年 8 月第 1 次印刷
字　　数	130 000		

物 料 号　22269-00